Ace Your Job Interview

By Gal Sivan

Table of Contents

Introduction

Thank you for purchasing this book! I am certain that it will live up to your expectations.

The behavioral interview aims to see if you will get along with your peers and whether you will be an asset to the company. It's a critical factor in the recruiting process. Companies try to assess a candidate's fit without knowing much about them. If you are not prepared, some of the questions will seem daunting.

With this book you will rock your behavioral interview and be a success. How do I know it? I know it because I have been there, and these are the techniques I used.

I have been on the job market many times, so I know how you feel. I have also sat at the other end of the table, asking the questions, thinking whether I should hire this person or not.

Now let's get to it!

General Advice

To start, you should have a buttoned-up answer for every behavioral question asked. They will ask many questions. You will want your answers to present your stories in a way that sounds natural, yet well prepared. To get to that point, you need to do the following:

1. Review all the questions in this guide, and develop answers based on your experiences. Jot down 1-3 examples from your life and work experience *per question.*

2. Once you have gone through all the questions, you will be ready to summarize your ideas. Summarize each example in 2-3 bullet points (more on that later).

3. Memorize all your bullet points for every question.

4. Get in front of a mirror or a webcam and rehearse your answer to each question. For best results, film yourself with the webcam and watch afterwards. Analyze your voice, flow and body language.

5. Do this for all questions, and rehearse over a few days.

One last thing. Great answers will usually have the following structure: situation->action->result. Here's what I mean:

1. *Situation*: A quick description of the situation you encountered.
2. *Action*: What you did. It's important to focus on the things that YOU did. Use the word "I" and not "we." Good interviewers will catch whether you ACTUALLY DID something, or are describing what you WOULD HAVE DONE. Use action verbs in past tense: "I led," "I managed," "I oversaw," "I improvised," "I sourced," (here's a comprehensive list: http://www.dummies.com/how-to/content/selling-yourself-in-a-resume-with-action-words.html).
3. *Result*: The result of your actions, successful or not. If not, then state what you learned from the result.

You should now be ready. Feel free to send me your best video (gal@aceyourinterview.info). I will not share it with anyone, but would love to see a bit of how and whom I was able to help. Good luck!

The Questions

1. Tell me about yourself

- Walk me through your resume
- Tell me a little bit about your career progress thus far
- Give me some highlights of your biography

Guide

This is your 1-minute pitch. It's your opportunity to make a lasting impression for the entire interview. When preparing your bullets, make each bullet THE highlight of what you did at every career stop. Your pitch should have the following structure:

1. Introduction catchphrase: answers the question, "why are you excited for this opportunity?"
2. Chronological order of work experience. Each bullet is the highlight of your experience.
3. How your skills will add value to this role, and why you should be considered for it.

Example Answer

I am excited about the opportunity to work in consulting because it's the next step in my career. I hope one day to get a general management role in digital media and technology.

While developing ACME's top game, I collaborated with cross-cultural teams to complete the project successfully. Before that I was a drummer with my country's most famous Hip-Hop band. Together we took the band from obscurity to a huge success. We sold platinum albums and performed in front of crowds of 50,000.

The business skills acquired at Nebraska University, combined with my creative and technological background, will enable me to add value by identifying problems and coming up with innovative solutions. Consulting is the natural choice for me. I want to play a key role in a challenging environment that will encourage my personal growth.

2. Why do you want this job?

- Why do you want to work in this industry?
- Why do you want to work in our company?
- What would you bring to our company and what do you want to get out of this job?

Guide

In this question the interviewer is looking to see if you did your homework. Did you research the company and the role you are applying for? It's important to insert the name of somebody you've spoken with. This shows that you are methodical and did your research. A good answer will have these components, in order:

1. The highlights of the company that you want to work for or the position that you want to fill. Using buzzwords internal to the company or industry will give you extra points.
2. A little bit about your background leading to...
3. What you bring to the table.
4. Why you are a great fit for this company and job.

Example Answer

I have always dreamed of working for ACME for many reasons. First, I love to learn. From speaking with John Doe, the Director of Business Development, I get a sense that there are amazing opportunities to develop here. Second, ACME is one of the leading firms in its industry. It utilizes cutting-edge technology and consists of a team that I would be proud to be a part of.

Technology and finance have intrigued me throughout my life. As a teenager I developed software that helped other kids make smart decisions with their allowance. In college I decided to major in economics, which led to my first job as an analyst at ABC. My biggest project was to find savings opportunities for one of our clients, based on financial statements and interviews. I succeeded in reducing costs by 35%. I got promoted to Senior Analyst and received a 20% raise. The project taught me to manage cross-functionally, and helped me improve my problem-solving skills. I believe these are crucial qualities for this position.

I feel that ACME has the mentality and the dynamic environment that I have always imagined working in. I am convinced I would be a valuable addition to the team!

3. What surprises you most about our company?

- What do you like most about our company?
- Why do you want this job?

Guide

This question is a variant of "Why do you want this job?" The interviewer wants to see how well you researched the company. She wants to know how passionate you are about the prospect of working there, and why you would like to work there. You can show here the amount of research that you did on this company. You can mention names of people you spoke with, and what kind of impression they made on you. Then you can say how the company's culture is in line with your values. Additionally, you can use content from your answer to "Why do you want this job?" (question 2). If you do that, switch your current job with the prospective job, making sure to drop a few buzzwords. Another way is to mention all the positive attributes you see about the company, and spin them as a surprise. You can answer the question as if it were "what impresses you about our company?" rather than "what surprises you about our company?"

<u>Example Bullets</u>

- *Great culture*: People took the time to speak with me and tell me more about the company.
- *Speed and efficiency*: Great response time from the HR department of the company. It means that the company culture praises efficiency, and invests in hiring well.
- *Laid back*: Although the company deals with complex business situations, the people seem to be laid back.
- *Charities*: I found out the company is involved in many charities that I didn't know were a priority for management.

<u>Example Answer</u>

Many things about your company surprised me. Here are a few that stand out. First, I was surprised by how people took the time to speak with me, and gave me a feeling that I was important to them. I realize that people are busy, and making time for candidates like me gives off a great impression. Both Adam Smith and John Doe explained the company's business to me, and the great plans that it has. Their attitude and passion toward their work impressed me.

Another thing that surprised me was to see how far you will go to make a customer happy. The people in the customer service group made me realize how dedicated you are to client success. This is a great sign, because a company that treats its clients so well often takes care of its employees.

4. How do you stand out among your peers?

Question Variants

- What are your three biggest strengths?
- Why should we hire you?

Guide

This is a question that is looking for you to describe your best qualities. When talking about success, it's always great to back it up with a detailed example. You can think of 1-3 qualities that make you a top performer, and then give an example for each. This is your opportunity to brag about yourself, but be careful not to sound too cocky. It's best to stick to the facts.

Example Bullets

- *Strength 1*: Leadership
  Use any one of your leadership stories in a situation->action->result structure. Here are some examples:
  - achieving superior results
  - generating more revenue because of an idea of yours

- getting people on board with your ideas
- helping people who struggle, etc.
- *Strength 2*: Creativity/thinking outside the box
  - *Situation*: I started a new job, and observed that the process to enter receipts into the computer was slow and full of errors. Many mandatory fields were unnecessary.
  - *Action*: I tinkered with the software, and realized it was possible to capture the same data with half of the effort. I showed this to my manager.
  - *Result*: My manager was excited, showed it to his manager, and the process was changed and I saved the company a lot of money.
- *Strength 3*: Conviction, dedication and discipline
  - *Situation*: I once had to deal with a client who was impatient and kept asking for additional support.
  - *Action*: I wanted to make the client happy since they had a big account with us. I spoke with the client at length to

understand the problem. They kept coming back to us with the same questions, and I wanted to understand why. I didn't say much, just listened to their concerns. In the end, it was clear that they were not using our system the right way. I explained how to do it right, and made sure they followed through.

- *Result*: The client was happy, and noted my patience and dedication to my manager. She proceeded to award me with an employee-of-the-month achievement.

5. What accomplishment gave you the most satisfaction?

<u>Question Variants</u>

- What is the coolest thing that happened to you in the last year?
- Tell me about a recent accomplishment you are particularly proud of and why

<u>Guide</u>

In this question the interviewer is trying to assess your passion, whether for work-related accomplishments or for life. Typical stories can include:

- Success in achieving a difficult task,
- A big accomplishment such as finishing a marathon,
- Successfully learning something new, etc.

The actual story doesn't matter if you show your passion, leadership, perseverance and resilience. You can also use this answer to discuss how you overcame a big challenge (see question 14).

Example Bullets

- *Situation*: I was a business analyst and I wanted to become a software engineer within my company. Transitions were difficult to achieve at my company.
- *Action*: I told my manager about my intentions, and started working for the new team on top of my regular job. I had to sell the new team's manager on my abilities.
- *Result*: I switched teams and have been making a great impact since.

Example Answer

I was a business analyst helping clients with their issues in certain situations. I loved writing code on the side, and wrote tools to help people in my group automate their processes. I felt software development was more exciting to me, and I wanted to be able to capitalize on that passion. Transitioning within a company, in any company, is not an easy thing to do. If you are a good employee, your manager is not incentivized to let you go. I had to be smart about it.

I spoke with my manager and told him I could add more value to the company from a new team, doing development work. I asked him if it was OK for me to carve out some of my personal time to work on the new team. He agreed. Next, I went to the other manager, whom I knew was desperate for engineers. I told him I could give him a few hours a week, and asked if he had any projects for me. He said he would think about it. I didn't wait, and I identified an opportunity to add value to the new team. I wrote a small tool that helped everyone be quicker. While the new manager was thinking about it, I worked 5 nights and a weekend to develop that tool. I emailed it to him, and he loved it. While I was still far from transitioning, I had my toe in the door.

He then came to me with an idea for a project. In the beginning I felt overwhelmed by it, because it wasn't anything like I did before. I didn't give up though, and took the time to study books and websites and teach myself the necessary skills to do it. I finished the project and aced it. My potential manager was beginning to see the value that I could add. He contacted my manager, and asked him if he could "borrow" me for 50% of the time every week. My manager was OK with it since he wanted to see me grow and develop and I had a great relationship with him. By the end of the quarter I switched teams.

This experience taught me that it's important to persevere and follow your passion. This is exactly what I am doing here in this interview with you, and what I am going to bring to the table.

6. What are your three biggest weaknesses?

Question Variants

- What is your greatest weakness?

Guide

This is a trick question. On the one hand, if you're too honest, you will scare the interviewer and will not pass. On the other hand, you still need to come up with a professional answer that addresses your weakness.

There are a few ways to approach this. My favorite approach is to pick a weakness which is a strength in disguise. It's simple to come up with these when you think about your strengths. Here are some examples (the weakness precedes the strength in parentheses):

- I tend to be slow (because I am detail-oriented and always deliver high quality work).
- I am a people-pleaser (which means I am easy and pleasant to work with).
- I tend to be a bit cocky (because I am confident in myself and I sell a lot).

- I am not the best listener (because I am smart and usually have the best ideas).
- I sometimes make mistakes (because I am quick and love to deliver my work ahead of deadlines).

Granted, some of these sound bad. With the correct spin, they can sound great and make you into a shiny candidate.

Once you have picked a couple of weaknesses, you need to structure your answer. As a rule, you want to structure your answer in two parts. The first part is a quick mention of your weakness, and the second part is how you are addressing the problem. You want to spin everything into a positive, inspiring answer. Remember, every weakness is an opportunity – you just need to convey that in the interview. You may be asked to talk only about one weakness, but you should always have a few ready. There are a couple of example bullets below. They should help you set up for a great answer.

<u>Example Bullets</u>

- Weakness 1: I tend to dive into the details and cover all bases.
  - *Weakness*: When given a task, I try to make sure every tiny corner is covered, and sometimes it slows me down.
  - *Hidden Strength*: The good side is that I always deliver high quality work.
  - *Remedy*: I have trained myself to stop every 10 minutes and ask myself whether what I was doing is serving the greater goal.
- Weakness 2: I am a people-pleaser. I tend to do things that I don't always want to do just to please others.
  - *Weakness*: I have a tendency to want people to like me, so I always try to please.
  - *Hidden Strength*: The good side is that I am likeable and pleasant to work with. Others love collaborating with me.
  - *Remedy*: Before I immediately say "yes" to others, I learned to ask myself if this

is what I should be doing now to get the job done.

7. Have you ever failed at anything?

Question Variants

- Tell me about a time when you didn't do so well.
- Tell me about a challenging situation you faced and did not achieve success.

Guide

In this question the interviewer wants to see that even if you fail at something, you learn for the next time. Many employers nowadays like to stress that if you don't fail you don't succeed. In this answer you need to show resilience – your ability to fail and bounce back up. The situation doesn't have to come from the workplace.

Example Bullets

- *Situation*: I wanted to get into a specific student organization to gain knowledge for my career.

- *Action*: I applied and didn't get in. I requested feedback on my application from anyone I could.
- *Result*: I learned how to write great applications. I even became a trainer and helped others with their career.

Example Answer

While in college, I wanted to get into InSite. InSite was a fellowship that provided consulting services to early-stage startup companies. I wanted in because it would have been a great experience to help others build something from the ground up. We had to submit a cover letter (since I was not raised in the States, I didn't know what that meant). We also had to write a short case analysis. I recall juggling a lot of my school work and activities just to make sure I got it right. I researched companies to write a case on, and stayed up late at night to come up with a compelling case study. I also had others review my cover letter. I was excited to submit everything on time. Unfortunately, I was not accepted.

This group was an amazing opportunity, and I missed my only chance to get in. I was disappointed. My initial reaction was of course to say "screw it" and move on. However, I did something completely different. I introduced myself to one of the InSite fellows, and had her explain how I could improve my application. She ended up reviewing a lot of my resumes and cover letters later on when I was applying for real jobs. All in all, even though I didn't get in, I made the best of this experience. I learned to write applications, resumes and cover letters, and even made it into a side business!

8. Tell me a little about what you do at work

- Tell me more about your current role
- How would you describe your job?

Guide

This may seem like a simple question, but when asked, it may take a while to come up with a coherent answer. Most people tend to just describe what they do in their role. This is not the right approach. Indeed, this question is yet another opportunity to showcase your achievements. To create a compelling answer, we again want to create mini-stories in bullet form. Some examples can be:

- Managing people to show leadership and management skills.
- Project work to show that you can understand the big picture and get along with different types of people.
- Work with software to show that you have technical and analytical skills.

- Anything that demonstrates your problem-solving skills.

Below are examples of qualities. Next to each example is a little story that demonstrates it through a job function. The structure of the answer should be:

- A general sentence about what you do.
- 3-6 sentences describing the skills you would like to highlight.
- A final sentence that gives a little extra, something that shows how you go above and beyond.

Example Bullets with Stories

- *Technical skills*: I am responsible for maintaining the network in our office. I am a member of a team of two people who maintain about 500 stations. We have a ticketing system, and on an average day I will tackle anywhere from 30 to 80 tickets. My main goal is to make sure that the network is always running and that all users are happy and can work. To me, if somebody is stuck waiting for something that I can't fix then I have failed at my job.

- *Analytical skills*: I work a lot with Excel, building complex models. These models help management understand strategic issues that the company is facing. They give management a clearer picture that will help them make a decision on the right course of action. Beyond my analytical skills, I make suggestions based on my own opinion. Many times management has incorporated my suggestions into the company strategy.

- *Managerial skills*: As a sales manager I have a team of five who report to me. I see my job as making sure that my team has everything it needs to move forward. I am always there to help them if they need me. I believe in hands-off management and I usually let my team roll until they hit an obstacle. It's also important to make sure that my people are feeling satisfied with the level of work that I give them. I try to divide the accounts based on my knowledge of the strengths of my employees. That way we all help move the business forward by leveraging our best skills.

- *Problem-solving skills*: As a customer support rep I got an average feedback score of 9.5 from hundreds of clients. I did this by asking them the right questions to identify underlying issues. When the answer was not immediately clear to me, I reached out to my colleagues to get help. After getting all the information this way, I was able to help many clients.

- *People skills*: In my previous job I started a movie club that got together once a month to watch films. My co-workers loved the idea and there was high participation. Later we even got funding from management to go out to the movies and make it a bigger company event. It helped improve our culture and the morale of the employees.

- *Organizational skills*: I have a system based on the book "Getting Things Done." I enter all my tasks in Evernote, and tag them with what, who, where and when. This system has helped me organize my work and change priorities on the fly. This is important because deadlines change all the time. It has kept me on track to finish my work on time and deliver it at a high quality.

- *Project management skills*: As a product manager I was in charge of many features of our product. I interacted with a cross-functional, global team. I had to coordinate meetings between time zones. I also defined objectives and success criteria and the processes to achieve them. I ensured that everyone was hitting milestones and that the projects were progressing.

- *Leadership ability*: When we had mass layoffs in the company, my team of five became three, and there was much more work to do. Morale was low due to the layoffs. I wanted to make sure that my people stayed focused and on track. I took a few steps. First, I called a team meeting to explain to everyone what was going on and hear their concerns. Then I called a 1-on-1 so people could be more candid about their concerns. I encouraged everyone to stay focused and not steer away from the added responsibility. I explained that hard times are the best times to get experience and learn. We all learned together how to deal with the situation. Everything went well and we kept delivering projects on time. We later actually expanded to be a larger team than before.

- *Creativity*: As an engineer at a music software company I initiated a 3-part course to teach engineers how to play drums. I also taught them how to read rhythm notes. This enabled them to better understand the needs of our clients. By coming up with this creative idea, I helped benefit the company. I was able to combine my passion for music and software development to do this.

9. What is your relationship with your manager? What is his role vs your role?

Question Variants

- Do you like your manager?

Guide

In this answer you want to highlight the best aspects of your relationship with your manager. Think about 3-4 key aspects that prove your dedication and your value to the company. Consider also showing that you are someone who is fun to be around.

The second part aims to see if you understand how the responsibilities break down between both of you. Will you not be stepping on your manager's toes? Try to show that you will be easy to manage, and will always go the extra mile. Show that you will do everything you can to make your manager's life easier. At the end of the day, your boss (and your potential boss) cares about one thing – your boss.

Example Bullets

- *Great relationship*:
    - I love helping him out and we have excellent 1-on-1's. He gives me good advice on my career progress, and I give him regular updates.
    - My manager always gives me the feeling that he is invested in my success.
    - My manager gives me a sense that he will give me coverage, even when things get sticky. This allows me to take more risks and achieve more.
    - My manager filters a lot of the noise that's trying to come in from above. He's great at prioritizing and picking out the important tasks I need to focus on.
- *Roles*: His role is to make sure we deliver on time, and divide the work among the people on his team. My role is to do my job as best as I can. Many times I help with allocating the work, and I usually do more than he requests from me.

<u>Example Answer</u>

My manager and I have a great relationship. First of all, I respect him a lot because he's smart. We both like to solve difficult programming questions from codinggame.com. We also like to do our 1-on-1's during lunch. He always has great advice for me and I get the feeling that he looks out for me and cares about my career development. At the same time, I do everything that I can to make him happy and make his life easier. I do much more than expected and try to venture out to areas outside of my direct expertise so I can both help and learn. I once helped him set up software on his computer that helped him save a lot of time.

With roles, he divides the work between the team members. I help him with that too. One time we had to finish a project for a big client under tight time constraints. My manager was busy with a different project, so he let me step up and take ownership. I divided the work and helped others on my team tackle their issues, involving him as little as possible. We were able to deliver on time, and he was pleased. My manager and I complement each other and I love working with him.

10. Pretend I am your friend and you are trying to sell me your job. Why should I become a ---?

<u>Question Variants</u>

- What do you like about your current job?

<u>Guide</u>

This question aims to see whether you like your job and why. Some people fall into a trap and discuss things they don't like – like their boss! You have to steer away from that. The person talking to you might become your boss! You want to list things that you love about your job and why you love them. It's also an opportunity to show why you are good. You need to give the interviewer the sense that you are going to be great and passionate about your career.

When praising your job, remember that you are leaving it for this new position. There is a fine line between naming the benefits of your job, and at the same time trying to leave it. Make sure the interviewer gets that you see the advantages of your current job, but are looking to grow.

This answer is not situation->action->result, but just a list of 3-5 things that you love and why. Mentioning good benefits or compensation is a given and not going to give you many points.

Example Bullets

- *Smart, engaging people*: I love to be around people who are smarter than me, because I get to learn a lot and improve and add more value.
- *Interesting projects/clients*: I love our clients' businesses. They are both interesting and challenging. It's an opportunity to see how people do X or Y. I love serving clients and some interesting things I did for clients were X, Y and Z.
- *Great culture*: There are many opportunities to learn. The company brings in experts on different subjects to talk about their fields. The people are generally nice, love to work hard but also know how to play hard.
- *Great career development opportunities*: Many training and learning opportunities. I get to interact with senior management on a daily basis. (Here you can provide a short situation-

>action->result example of such a successful interaction).

<u>Example Answer</u>

There are a few things I love about my current job and about my company. First of all, it's a great place to work. The people are smart and there is an opportunity to learn something new all the time. When I look at my skills a year ago and now, I can hardly believe it's the same person! When I came in I didn't know what a balance sheet looked like, or how to use Excel, and now I am writing business plans!

Another thing that I love about our company is the culture. There is a heavy learning culture in our company. They bring outside speakers to give us interesting talks.

The third thing I love is getting to know our clients and their businesses inside and out. We get to interact with clients on a daily basis, and I love giving great service and getting great feedback. Getting an occasional thank-you note makes it even better.

Finally, there is a lot of opportunity to develop here. There is flexibility to move between positions, and I think the company values my work and rewards me for it. I would recommend my job to anyone on any given day!

11. What do you do outside of work?

Question Variants

- Do you have a personal goal outside of work?

Guide

This question aims to assess if you are a well-rounded person. It doesn't mean you should get carried away and get too personal. It's rather an opportunity for you to show that you are creative, goal oriented, and can be a leader. Is there any value you can add by thinking outside the box? Have you had any ideas or led any interesting projects? Have you set a personal goal and achieved it? This question doesn't need a situation->action->result structure, but it's always better to use it. A great strategy here is to actually refer to some personal goal that you have outside of work and talk about that. Maybe you finished a well-known hike (i.e. the Appalachian Trail). Maybe you competed in a marathon, or learned a language. Maybe you have been writing a blog. There are many ways you can show valuable skills by your outside activities. Check out the example below for even more ideas.

Example Answer

There are a couple of things that I like to do outside of work. I am passionate about music and I play the guitar. I have a band with some friends, and we sometimes jam together on the weekends. We also perform covers at a local bar. I am also passionate about cooking. I like to find international recipes online, invite friends and cook for them. Last time, I made a special arugula salad with Italian cheese and it was a hit. One thing I also do is volunteer teaching inner-city children about coding. One of my students actually landed an internship in company XYZ! I also practice and teach yoga when I can. There is a children's hospital nearby, and I volunteer there on weekends teaching yoga. You should see the smiles on these kids' faces when we finish our sessions.

12. Do you have a personal goal outside of work?

- Tell me about a personal goal you've set for yourself in the past 1-2 years.
- What do you do outside of work?

Guide

Like question 11, this one is trying to assess whether you are both driven and well rounded. Typical examples include:

- Finishing a marathon
- Finishing a hike
- Learning a language
- Learning a new skill, such a musical instrument, painting, cooking, coding, etc.
- Raising money for a charity
- Volunteering

Your answer can be a situation->action->result, or a description of the goal and how you will reach it.

Example Bullets

- I decided to learn French, and set a goal to read a French children's book in 1 year.
- I found a great app called DuoLingo, voted the best educational app on iTunes.
- I started taking 5 lessons a day, and doing homework.
- I started reading the book - one page per day.

Example Answer

I have always been curious to learn another language. I want to better understand other cultures and have a better time traveling. I decided to study some French because I love the culture, the country and the food. To be accountable, I set a measurable goal: finish reading a French children's book within a year.

After some research, I found out that there was an amazing free app on the iPhone that teaches languages. I started using the app and taking lessons. The app proved to be as great as I heard. I did about five lessons a day on my subway commute to work. In the beginning it didn't feel like much, but I stuck with it and did my homework and followed the lessons.

One of my strongest qualities is that I am disciplined, and I did this for the first six months.

As I got more comfortable with the language, I found a children's book that had about 150 pages. I realized that if I finished a single page a day I would be able to finish the book in six months. I kept with it, finished the book and now I am conversant in French!

13. Tell me about a time you showed leadership skills

Question Variants

- Tell me about a challenge that you had to handle at the workplace.
- Give an example of a time when you had to deal with someone who wasn't pulling their weight.
- Describe a time when you've confronted an obstacle.

Guide

This is an opportunity to discuss your success stories, either as a leader or an individual. In extreme cases where you don't have a success story, you can use a failure. That is, detail what you learned from the experience, and how you improved. The story can also talk about leadership without managing a team of people. It can describe a situation where you emerged as a leader because of how you acted.

Example Bullets

- *Situation*: I participated in a fundraiser for 20 families, but realized that I could do much more.
- *Action*: The next year I did everything on my own. I identified people who needed help, set a goal for the fundraiser, and planned all the steps to achieve it.
- *Result*: I ended up helping 6 times the number of needy families and elderly people as last year.

Example Answer

Last year I joined a small volunteering project that a colleague of mine started. It involved packing food for the holidays and distributing it to 20 needy families. We raised $1000 for this from colleagues who donated for this project. After participating once, I realized we could do much more.

This year, I decided to do something bigger. First I needed a target audience for my project, so I involved a friend of mine who was a social worker for the city. She identified a group of 120 elderly holocaust survivors living in a government home. I then committed to helping them get great products for the holidays. I still didn't know how I was going to make it happen, but I took the risk.

To figure out my target for this project, I had her ask them what it was they most needed. She came back to me with a list. Next, I recruited friends to each act as my agent in their workplaces, and collect donations. A friend introduced me to a manager at a large food retailer, and I negotiated a big discount for the cause.

When the day came, I headed there with some work friends. We loaded up cars with boxes and went to the home to distribute them. Altogether we raised $5000, helping 30 families and 120 elders.

Since I wasn't a manager at the time, I found this project to be a great avenue for my managerial skills. I learned to take risks, improvise when necessary, and most of all I learned that if there is a will then there is a way.

14. Tell me about a recent crisis you handled

Question Variants

- Tell me about a challenge that you had to handle at the workplace.
- Give an example of a time when you had to deal with someone who wasn't pulling their weight.
- Describe a time when you've confronted an obstacle.

Guide

In this question the interviewer is looking to see how you are able to cope with adversity and conflict. Do you easily give up when confronted with challenges? Are you able to handle them and achieve results? If not successful, did you learn anything that will prepare you better for next time?

Adversity at a workplace can arise from many situations. They might involve relationships between employees or employee-manager relationships. They could relate to clients, or impossible demands imposed by them. They can also arise from tight time constraints. The goal of this question is to see how you can handle all that. You need to show that you maintain a positive, calm attitude and control the situation.

The format of your answer is again situation->action->result. Try to first sketch out your answer in bullets, and then build it around them, adding more detail.

Example Bullets

- *Situation*: We were given a task to do under time constraints, and one of the members of the team was not cooperating.
- *Action*: I pulled him aside and gently asked what was holding him up, and if there was anything I could do to help. He said that he had a technical issue which was too difficult, and he didn't want to deal with it. I offered to trade tasks with him.
- *Result*: The project finished on time. I learned that when there is a problem, it's good to communicate and not freak out.

Example Answer

When I was working as a software engineer for ACME, we had a task to complete under tight time constraints. I don't remember the exact details, but we had to figure out a difficult technical problem. They asked me to lead it, and told me I could use the help of another engineer. I was not his manager, but I was on the hook to solve this problem.

After a quick discussion, the other engineer and I decided to divide and conquer the task. He took one piece and I took another. Later on, I checked in with him to make sure that he was not having any issues. When I asked him how it was going he said that he wasn't working on it and that he hadn't done anything.

At this point I realized that if he wasn't going to do his part then we would not be able to roll out the fix on time. I needed to act fast because we had already lost some time. I pulled him aside, and gently asked him what was holding him up, and if there was anything I could do to help. He wasn't too motivated, and he said that his piece of the project was too difficult. It didn't sound like he wanted to deal with it. I said, "OK, I understand. Let's see if we can do something to change this." I offered to trade tasks. He preferred my part, so he thought it was a good idea, and he seemed more motivated after that. I worked on his piece of the project and we both brought it to completion just in time.

I learned that it's always better to communicate early. I also learned that there is a logical reason why people don't always do what you expect them to do. By empathizing with my colleague, and trying to help him out, I was able to ensure the fix went out on time.

15. Tell me about a time you worked with someone you didn't want to work with

Question Variants

- Do you like your boss?
- Tell me about a time when you didn't like your boss.
- Can you give me an example of a difficult interaction with a colleague?

Guide

This question can be a trap, but also an opportunity to show your dedication and your value to the company. Remember, your goal in an interview is to always show that you add value, even when you face challenges. Many people fall into the trap in this question by admitting that they don't like to work with someone. You should NEVER ever complain about a colleague or your manager! If I am your future boss and you are complaining to me about your manager, why would I want to hire a bad apple to my team? Also, there are always unpleasant people at any organization. You never know when that next person will turn up, so you need to prove that you can handle any situation. You can't rely on everything being rosy. Keep your positive attitude, and show how you handled the situation in a smart manner. Portray yourself as a giver. Show that you are always ready to sacrifice your own time or energy, and at times your pride, to get the project done. You don't have to get along with everyone, but you have to show how you bring tasks to a successful completion. The example will show what I mean.

Example Bullets

- *Situation*: I was assigned to work on a project with a person who had a bad reputation in the company for being difficult.
- *Action*: I came with an open, positive attitude to the project. I over-communicated with my colleague to ensure I got what their preferred mode of work was. I also asked her what she wanted me to do. I negotiated with her my preferred way to do things, and we made a compromise and met on middle ground.
- *Result*: We completed the project successfully.

<u>Example Answer</u>

When I was a consultant, I got assigned to a team that consisted of a manager and a couple of associates like me. One of these associates had a bad reputation in the company as someone who was difficult to work with. As soon as work started, I realized that she was indeed quite difficult. She would freak out and yell, and always add unnecessary stress, instead of getting the work done. I had to do something, not only for my sake, but also for the sake of the team.

During one of the days I asked her if I could buy her some coffee so we could talk. She agreed. I asked her about her preferred mode of working on the project, and what her working style was. I shared with her my mode and suggested a way for us to share the workload and divide and conquer. She agreed, we worked out a plan, and brought the project to successful completion.

16. Tell me about a time where you annoyed someone with your actions

- Tell me about a disagreement you had with someone and how you resolved it.

Guide

In this question the interviewer wants to see if you are someone who is comfortable to work with. This question is a trap to make you reveal your bad qualities to the interviewer. The best way to avoid these types of traps is not to meddle with your negative qualities. Just don't go there and avoid the issue. You do this by giving a positive spin on anything negative that you could say about yourself. There are some methods to give a positive spin to something:

- Mention that you are improving on it and it's not a problem anymore.
- You can mention the strategies that you are taking to address a situation that used to exist in the past.

- You can say that even though your actions annoyed someone, they were necessary for finishing the task.

Example Bullets

- *Situation*: I got involved in a project with two key contradicting approaches. I was a proponent of one way, and a colleague wanted to do the other way. When the team discussed it, most were leaning toward my way, and the other person became annoyed.
- *Action*: I pulled him aside and told him that I didn't mean to annoy him. I let him know that while we were using my approach we will incorporate many of his suggestions. I even gave him some examples too.
- *Result*: The person was happy and we brought the project to a successful conclusion.

Example Answer

A few months back corporate asked us to do XYZ. There were only two possible approaches to make it happen. I could see that one option was much better than the other, for many reasons. At a team discussion I said we should go with that option, and I listed the reasons I thought were relevant. Another person on the team had an opposite opinion, but his reasoning was flawed. I did not call him out on that, but tactically guided the conversation to where people could see why I was correct. It didn't help, and he became agitated with where the conversation was going.

I realized that the team couldn't continue working together like this with him. I knew I had to do something to remedy the situation. I invited him for coffee. I explained to him that he had great ideas, and I could see why he thought his approach was better. I assured him that the success of the project was top of mind for me. I told him that we could include many of his ideas in the project. I gave him an example of how one idea of his could already work.

We ended up having a great relationship over the course of the project and we brought it to a fantastic ending.

17. Tell me about a situation where you decided to take a risk

Question Variants

- Tell me about a time when you acted against the opinion of your manager.
- Tell me about a time when you had to think out of the box and make a difficult decision.

Guide

This question is an opportunity to show leadership, so any good leadership story will do. You can spin the story in a way that shows you were taking a risk. Some examples may include:

1. A time when you decided to go against what your team thought, and you ended up being right.
2. A time when you saw an opportunity in your life, and decided to go for it. This could include going back to school and quitting your job or starting a new business.
3. A time when you went against what everybody told you. Maybe your parents wanted you to

become one thing, and you decided to become something else.

Your story doesn't have to end up as a success, but if you don't succeed, you need to show in your answer what you learned from the experience.

Example Bullets

- *Situation*: I had a comfortable job as a software engineer for a big company. I had great prospects for promotion and everything was going well. Despite that, I didn't feel satisfied, and wanted to grow. I wanted to use my creativity and leadership skills.
- *Action*: I decided to quit my job and go back to school.
- *Result*: I got my MBA and this gave me leverage for a career change. I am now a product manager working in a cutting-edge technology company.

A few years back I had been working for company XYZ as an engineer. I loved my job, but I always felt that I could do more. Things were going well, and my manager even told me that soon I would be up for a promotion. Something inside didn't feel right though. I felt I wasn't using all my skills, and I wanted to switch into a role with more responsibility. I am creative and love working with people.

After some thought, I realized maybe it was time to go back to school. It was a difficult decision because I would not earn money for a few years. Also I wasn't sure about getting out of the job market. It's easy to get out but not as easy to come back. Fast forward two years, a whole new world opened up! So many new jobs became available because of my degree! I learned that it's never comfortable to take risks, but sometimes it's the only way to make progress. It's always worth it, because even if you fail, you still learn something from your failure.

18. Can you tell me about a time you tried something new in your organization that had not been done before?

Question Variants

- Tell me about a situation where you decided to take a risk.
- Tell me about a time when that you had to think out of the box and make a difficult decision.
- I know this is one of your strengths, but tell me about a time when you've done something innovative.

Guide

This is like question #17, except that it focuses on something you did in your own organization. Examples include:

- Taking on a new initiative
- Improving a process
- Getting people to volunteer outside of work

Your answer can reflect actions you did as a manager or as an individual contributor. This question works with situation->action->result.

Example Bullets

- *Situation*: I realized that while everyone was doing their job, nobody knew what people liked doing outside of work.
- *Action*: I started a monthly lecture by workers based on their interests and hobbies, like TED Talks.
- *Result*: Office morale improved and everyone is now looking forward to these talks. They turned into a thing that creates project ideas and help the company in its strategic efforts.

Example Answer

When I started my current job, I noticed everyone had other interests. People volunteered, had hobbies, charities, etc. but nobody was sharing this knowledge. I thought it might be beneficial if people shared their interests and expertise. I have seen this done in other companies, so thought it would be great to take this initiative. It wasn't easy. The idea was only in my head, and it was difficult to convince management to carve out time for such an activity. The benefit to the company was not immediately clear. I had to prove how this will actually boost employee performance and morale.

I set to work. I collected research data demonstrating the positive effects these activities have on production. Then I prepared slides to show exactly what I was planning to do. I explained why I thought it would be great for the company, and I backed it by my research data. When it was ready, I presented this to my manager, who loved the idea, and told me to reach out to the head of HR. He loved the idea as well, and we ended up implementing it successfully!

19. Tell me about a disagreement you had with someone and how you resolved it

Question Variants

- Tell me about a time when you annoyed someone with your actions.

Guide

Here you want to show that despite a disagreement you were able to bring a project to completion. It's OK to show a disagreement. You just need to talk about actions you took to resolve it. It's even more compelling to show that you were also able to get the other party on board with your idea! Moreover, show that they took action to help YOU get it done. We have some examples of that with other questions. Your answer here can show leadership or dealing with a non-cooperative colleague as well. This is a classic situation->action->result structure.

Example Bullets

- *Situation*: My manager gave an me assignment to write code, and suggested doing it in a certain way. When we discussed it, I realized there could be a more efficient way to do it. She disagreed.
- *Action*: I implemented the task both ways, devoting personal time to the extra work. I showed her that by doing it my way, she will be able to show the code to her manager and look great.
- *Result*: My manager ended up agreeing with me and adopting my idea. When we presented it to her boss I gave her full credit for coming up with the whole method.

Example Answer

As software engineers, we have a lot of decisions to make on the architecture of how code should work. There are many ways to implement the same spec. Selecting a design has trade-offs on speed, memory, code scalability and ease of maintenance. My manager asked me to develop a new feature, and she was in favor of a certain method. I realized that there were a few gaps in her idea, because of a few assumptions that didn't make sense. At first I tried to show this to her, but she disagreed with me, and told me to build the feature the way she asked. I agreed, of course, and went to work.

I love working with my manager and I learn a lot from her, but I was still convinced that she was wrong on this point. Instead of trying to prove her wrong, I worked harder, and put in a couple of nights. I ended up building the feature both ways. When everything was ready I told my manager what I did, and she was open to checking out both solutions. Believe it or not, she was impressed with what I did and ended up choosing my implementation over hers. When we presented this to our group manager I gave her full credit for coming up with this solution. He was happy and I was happy to make my boss look good.

20. Tell me about a time when you had to do something that you didn't want to do

Question Variants

- Were you ever asked to do something that you didn't feel like doing?
- Tell me about a time when you felt your values were challenged.

Guide

This is a common question, because it's trying to see if you will do any task, even if it's not exactly what you want to do. They want to see if you have a can-do attitude. There are many examples of disgruntled employees. You may have heard people complain about their jobs, saying they had to do things they were not hired for. This is the kind of worker that companies try to avoid, because they need people with a can-do attitude. This is what you need to show. There are many stories that you can pick here:

- My manager asked me to work on a project that I was not interested in, but I still aced it.

- My manager asked me to work with someone I didn't like, but I went and did it and we aced the project.
- I was going through personal issues, with no mood to do anything, but I still overcame it and did great.
- My manager asked me to do something I believed was wrong for the team/company.
- My manager asked me to do something that I didn't know anything about. I felt lost and didn't like it, but I learned, became an expert and did well.

We already have stories for some of the above examples in previous questions. As a general rule, you must show that you are loyal even if you disagree with the task. Whether you're wrong or right, every manager likes to ask for things once, and then see them finished. In any case you always need to show that first you do what they tell you. You can say that you questioned the assignment, but aced it despite that. Then you can add that you took extra time to show why you thought it was not the right thing to do. I am going to use the fourth example to show you what I mean. This is a classic situation->action->result question.

<u>Example Bullets</u>

- *Situation*: My manager asked me to do something that I felt was wrong for the company.
- *Action*: I did everything he asked me to the letter, despite my concerns. In my free time I prepared a presentation for him to argue my case.
- *Result*: He was happy with my work, and was even more pleased with my presentation. While he disagreed with my rationale, it gave him some ideas on how we could retain most of our business.

<u>Example Answer</u>

When I was in sales, my manager asked me to go after some client. I didn't think it was the type of client we wanted in our portfolio. I realized that once some of our long-time clients found out, they would stop doing business with us. Even so, I went after this account just as my manager requested of me. Though I expressed my thoughts when he gave me the assignment, I still went ahead and did it. At the same time, I decided to make sure that he understood why I didn't think it was a good idea. I stayed in a couple of lunches so I could make a deck to present my arguments for why I thought it wasn't the best idea. After a while, I approached my manager and asked to present my ideas to him. While he didn't agree all the way, he could see my point. Furthermore, it gave him some ideas on what we could do if our veteran clients indeed left us.

21. Tell me about a time when you felt your values were challenged. How did you feel? What did you do? How did others react?

<u>Guide</u>

This is definitely a tough one. On one hand, you want to show that you are ethical. On the other, you want to show that you are loyal to your manager. This is an opportunity to show your values to the interviewer. You can also help them understand that your values are in line with the values of what the company is after.

Don't worry if you don't have an example for actual ethical issues. You could spin a work-challenge story into a story where somebody challenged your values. You could take our story of a difficult colleague, and say he challenged your values and your work ethic.

Another example you could use is a time when you had to let go of someone because they did something unethical. Stay away from stories about when you were asked to do something unethical yourself. This is because it could take you into muddy territory if you're not careful. No one would like to hire somebody they can't trust on their team. Even if they are evil. This is sad but it's true. Remember, the boss only cares about one thing – the boss.

Example Bullets

- Our sales manager told us to research and come up with sales leads. He asked us not to buy any online because there were privacy issues with these vendors.
- My colleague wanted to still go online and buy them because it took a lot of leg work to source our own leads.
- I managed to talk him out of it.
- Another guy did the same thing, got caught and fired. My friend thanked me.

Example Answer

In sales, we're always looking to increase our market share and get more clients for our company. Our manager decided it was time to expand our client base. He wanted us to source leads for him. He also asked us not to buy any leads online, because our company had privacy concerns. It's not right to guarantee clients full privacy with one hand, and then buy shady data with the other. It's just bad business.

For us this meant that we would have to scour phone books and make many calls, without selling anything. One of my colleagues didn't agree with our manager, and decided to buy leads online anyway. He let me in on his intentions. I didn't like it. Beyond challenging my values, it was dangerous, and against the instructions of our manger.

I grabbed my friend aside, and explained to him all this. I convinced him that even if he got the leads and wasn't caught, the upside is small. This was just a thankless job we had to do, without commission, but we had to do it. I was happy that he listened to reason and followed my advice.

A couple of days after we submitted our leads, somebody indeed got caught buying leads online. They fired that person on the spot. My friend thanked me for talking some reason into him, and I was happy that I took the long, but honest road.

22. Tell me about a time when you helped out a colleague

Guide

This is a great opportunity to show leadership. You can tell stories about helping somebody on your team who was struggling to finish their task. You can talk about how somebody needed help on a personal level where you just took the time to listen to her. You could also tell how you mentored a new employee and helped them succeed. This question works well with the situation->action->result structure.

Example Bullets

- *Situation*: We were working together on a big project, and a colleague was struggling and not making any progress. People were starting to get annoyed with her, and she got frustrated and didn't know what to do.
- *Action*: I pulled her aside and asked her if there was anything I could help with. She told me she didn't have clear instructions, and was too shy to ask. She thought people would think she was not smart.

- *Result*: After I helped her she aced her piece, we all finished the project on time and she gained the respect of her peers.

Example Answer

Our team was given a large project to work on. There were four of us and a manager. The manager was not always clear, and I had had difficulties understanding her in the past. The deadline was tight, just a couple of days, so we had to work around the clock to finish the project. We had to do a complex analysis for a client. When we started, we decided to check in twice a day to make sure that everyone was on track. In our second check-in it became clear that one of us was not making the expected progress on her piece. We were about to fall behind, and the team began to get annoyed with her. I decided to see what I could do to help.

First I spoke with all the team members one by one to assuage their fears about the fate of the project. I explained that if worse came to worst, we would all be able to pull our weight and get it done with a bit of extra work. Of course none of us preferred to go that route, but it was one of our options.

Next, I approached the troubled colleague to understand her situation in a compassionate manner. I asked her what was holding her back, and reassured her that everything she said stayed between us. She told me that she just didn't understand the instructions our manager gave, and she was too shy to ask. She thought the manager or some people on the team would judge her as slow or incapable. I was a little bit more experienced and I knew how to work with our manager. I understood the situation and was ready to help. I asked her for her instructions and together we figured out what was necessary to do to complete her piece.

After this conversation, she did better than all of us! The project was a success and she went on to become known and respected in the company.

Bonus Section: Questions to Ask

Usually behavioral interviewers leave some time at the end of the interview for Q&A. This is another great opportunity to show interest in the position and the company. Here are some questions that I like:

- What do you like best in your job?
- What do you think is the best thing about this company?
- Can you walk me through a typical day for someone at this role?
- Where do you see the company going in the next 5 years?
- I'd love to know more about the company culture.
- What do you think makes this company better than its competitors?
- What's your timeline for a decision?

www.ingramcontent.com/pod-product-compliance
Lightning Source LLC
Chambersburg PA
CBHW060409190526
45169CB00002B/816